My Nights in C

ACKNOWLEDGEMENTS

Thanks to the editors of the following publications where these poems, sometimes in earlier versions, first appeared: *Agenda*, *The Boy Under the Water* (The Many Press, 1989), *Exeter Poetry Prize Anthology* (Odyssey, 1996), *Navis*, *Other Poetry*, *Oxford Poets 2002: An Anthology* (Carcanet, 2002), *Poetry London*, *PN Review*, *Poetry Review*, *Poetry Wales*, *Quadrant*, *The Rialto*, *Staple*, *The Tabla Book of New Verse*, *Thumbscrew*, *The Times Literary Supplement*, *Tying the Song* (Enitharmon Press, 2000).

Thanks are also due to Hawthornden Castle for the International Fellowship during which some of these poems were written.

CONTENTS

An Angel Entered the Picture

Years of careful work had made
the illusion perfect.

A stroke of grey was like the sky
divided from brown by a long neat line

we believed was the horizon.
Up and down were like the fixed stars.

Rocks lay still. In angled shadows
houses looked exactly sharpened.

Trees stood rooted to the spot
as if the law of gravity

had been a religion, then stepped back
in graduated sizes to the smaller

thinner blue as we knew they would.
The picture resembled life so closely

mist rose straight up from the lawn.
Then an angel entered.

Red went right through to the centre
where there were two hearts.

Beating together, main arteries linked
in intense traffic, the red

filling with red and rising
even to the words on our lips.

Remember how we saw
the frame peel away, the air glisten

like daylight without its skin.
And how, leaping out of bed,

we threw the window open to find
a breeze was blowing.

THE NIGHT KITCHEN

Outside extinct stars hang
like scrunched-up letters thrown
around the floor. The earth is poised
on a hook above the sink.
An enormous sponge sits planetary and alone
in its enamel dish. So if I notice

a cracked glass face-down needs chucking out,
the draining-board is chipped by something
dropped last year, the forks all look
faintly yellow between their prongs –
why do my arms wrapped in mist in the Fairy Liquid
feel the long warm pull of the tide?

Why is it suddenly all
a darkness of islands in oceans, the inconstant soap
a slab of light slipping between my fingers
like a moon? And if the folded
dishcloth rises to a pinnacle of hope
against an embroidery of midnight-blue,

and if the bubbles coming on and going out
range themselves in a white ring big
as the Crab Nebula, and if I'm floating
inches above the ground, the pocket in my apron
growing into a pouch so large that it could hold
Medusa's head, J-cloths flapping

from my heels like the wings of Mercury,
and through the hazy half-dark I begin to see
a constellation in a drift of dust,
puddles on the floor big enough to hold the Milky Way –

will you keep the earth's poles
together between your firm hands, administer
the law of gravity, and hold
onto all the rattling atoms of the world?

THE SUN AT THE TABLE

It's these freak storms.
Shining like a lunatic
your smile plays hell

with all astronomy. That cold
luminous arc, the blinding white
ellipse. Like watching a drop

of water always about to fall.
It's the door of a safe slowly
swinging closed on a million

dollar room, spectacularly lit,
a black box shut in the ground
hiding its information like a skull.

But look both ways. Flames play
over the backs of your hands.
Even as we sit faces facing,

bushes break apart and it comes
out into the open. Now it openly
conceals its blazing secret

behind a cloud. Round a bend
a brisk traveller vanishes
down a path like a broken thread.

A few words spoken with calm.
And in the weedy lost mood
of the sea I can just make out

a pale green room rising and falling
near the bottom. There are two
small people sitting at a table.

WOLF IN THE KITCHEN

You wait crouched down behind
your eyes, so deeply out of reach
I frighten you by moving
my hand too quickly.
Funny how we can still sit
as usual in the empty kitchen.

Motionless talk hangs
in dry particles suspended in space,
the restless knives and plates never
seem to relax, the glasses are full
of promises grown small.

And there is a wind crossing a field felt
lightly against the face.
You are a wolf stepping gingerly

from a wood. The sides of your body
panels of light, your essential tongue,
your perfect claws and teeth shut in.
A little mercury grows
brighter and brighter, your hunger rages

like a tear. Shining silently you burn
inside your unfathomable fur.
Ears abashed, eyes round
and scared. (Keep still or you will startle him.)
You are stepping gingerly from a black
wood into a wide yellow field.

Now move slowly, move
without moving, and I am as yellow
as the field itself,
as black as the wet trees' bark,
a nothing in the air, unseen, a pause,
a different scent. Drops of saliva stick
to the hairs around your mouth.
Please come and let me feed you.
I hold out my hand
like a beggar and you are released.
It is the deep red time of the body,
I offer it as meat.

PANTOMIME

This is when we lift the lid
off the box, take out the flat
brown suit, then gravely as a crown

loop the tunnel of the neck
over our heads, unroll the four
rumpled legs, step in and run the zip
up the stomach. This is better

than we thought: the bronze rump
shining in the sun, the velvet lips,
the curve of the intelligent neck.
Sit back and watch the perfect

half-wit smile spread. Swaying
gently like a milk-float
(to light applause) tiny
goose-steps locked

we tinker up onto the stage.
I spill a long wet tongue
from the mouth. You aim a graceful
squirt of milk from the penis

(a standing ovation) push
a spot-lit hand through to wag the tail.
Sausages are gliding in a pink heap
onto the floor. We paw the earth,

lower the dynamic head and take
several fences. Now we're floating
high over the steep hills and far away.
Yes it is. No it's not – a large

crumpled heap of corduroy on the floor.
Don't miss it. Our double act
zipped up together in the semi-dark,
heads I win, tails you lose,

is for this limited season only.
We collapse the legs, rub out
the eyes, take up the ears by the roots.
But hold on. The stable-door is locked.

This bolting horse is a cuckoo
in the nest, a marching army of occupation,
an enormous tongue in the mouth.
It will run and run.

WAITING FOR THE PRINCE

From the top of the sky the sun
alights and settles
a deep white on the chosen moment
and sleeps like glass.

The table is set like a throne.
Stuck on one note tuned and tuned,
it's summer now
all day long, only the table

is sharply tapering, stretching out
like elastic, a space, impassable as sand,
to where he sits as silent
as the Sleeping Beauty waiting

perfectly for the Prince.
And while we both still sit,
in the sleep of a hundred years
and wait for his awakening kiss,

could that be him? Could the faint
rustle in the hawthorn hedge be his
penetrating hands, the sudden
moist sting in the air, his tongue?

Or, the cabbage-white flitting
absently from place to place
among the buddleia, his lips
never quite coming in to land?

Dog Rose

Out of the foliage they half-appear,
fragile, fresh-made, crying,
completely filling the tree.
A manic white tumult in the garden.
The dog rose is losing its head,
teeming with mad thoughts thick as bubbles.
Some contain little iridescent pictures
of you. You are just running out,
you say, to post a letter. A tiny
sound on the other side of the house
as a door is carefully slammed.
Look quickly: they slip
the mind and break apart. As if
nothing had happened,
the tree is engrossed in its leaves.

TREE-POEM FOR APOLLO

My fingertips are planning their escape.
There go my hands up over my head,
they ease out ten long buds,

each one sticking out its tongue:
a wet green stalk
and a leaf. I am speaking to you now

only through the vocabulary of leaves:
how they are open and continually open,
the rush of sap

where the stem begins
the too-much-detail of their veins,
the daft shine on their faces

as they fall all over themselves
to see the sun,
the way they have of blurting out *green! green!*

All these things I say out loud,
but, for you, I disappear into an instant
tunnel of bark, furred-over, hidden.

How can my body go
into such abeyance that I become
only a thin blonde ring of growth,

so far down in the centre of the trunk,
I'm lost as the small private O
shining at the bottom of a well?

Deep as an animal brain
ticking its secret

on unknown frequencies inside
the smooth stroked head
under your hand.

LANDING ON THE SUN

A small sun fallen to the ground,
your hand rests on the cluttered table
and grows cool. Still impossible to look
at it directly: the blinding mathematics
of each bent finger glowing

round and hot as the segments
of a baby's arm. Asleep
in a pool of ash, the curve of your hand
smiles like a sickle.
While I, in a lead suit

against the radiation, stare dazed
from a safe distance (the other side
of the table) at the long bunched fingers
looking as seductive as fruit
hanging from a tree just out of reach.

Your white hand is a star a child would want
to pencil in and out, in and out,
to keep pinned to a wall. Better not let
the angle of your thumb and index finger look
as though I might insert my fingers there:

a space to park outside tall buildings
as it's getting dark. A paper cup
is knocking desperately against a kerb,
the house has all the lights switched on
waiting for you to come home.

in the sea of debris, balled-up napkins, capsizing cups
or I might try to navigate towards it,
fetch up alongside and tie my hand

sideways to yours like a dock.
Don't let your fingers fit their taut lines
and bent joints together with such subtle

engineering that they lead me to a slippery
ladder where, vanishing into the water,
the black rungs swarm, lose all known

geometry, thicken like a plot
I can no longer follow. If so many shadows
banked up around your fingers, they would multiply

like the jealousy of a man who can't imagine
where she's been; be carried to more places
than the decimals on the blackboard at school

I'd sit at the back of the class unable to understand.
But if you let even the smallest light
escape from the core of your hand so that it

glows like an electric fire,
the orange bars on the horizon might make me see
the sky looking down at me kindly

from the corner of its eye. Better not
wait there and fade to a fingernail of light,
or my eyes would cling like a drowning man

to this small picture of your hand
seeing it slowly shrink
to nothing but itself: neat, white, hard.

But stay a little. Let's see its whole
parade up ahead hanging out pink banners
and clouds. Be, for a moment, like the sun

to keep me from running out of light,
from falling like a red undone button
no one has seen dropping under the table.

Yes and No

Even before you were born you
lived in her intricate hands.

She would leave them
open like messages

saying yes and saying no,
two unfolded maps of a country

where the sea behaved like theft
and disappeared or loomed

round and white, sent
sheets of rapid milk

across the sand, but only
for a moment, then tugged them back,

smoothing and smoothing a new place
fresh as a sting.

Even before you were born you
lived in her absent-minded

smile. A surprise appearance
of the sun had nothing

on the way it spilled
into a sudden arc stretched out

to hold you. Or let you go.
Smiling her smile. And there it was:

the open secret she wore inside out
showing its label by mistake.

Even before you were born you
lived in her chambered heart.

Two-up, two-down, when you
were wrapped up small

as a glimpse, the double doors
swung you both ways, beat

you in their pulse, carried
you abruptly on the tide

of their in and out, cradled you
and whispered cold in the warm air.

MUTE

Little tree as empty as a house
when your mother is not at home,
few or yellow or promising
they will come back, your syllables
are loose circles blown about
barely forming words, your leaves
amount to nothing without her saying
*You look lovely standing there
in your hair and your dress.*

The Pulse

If the heart is a house my parents
live there separated by a wall.

Tall rooms are secretly linked
by long muscular stairs, a pyramid

of light I travel up to the point
of their joining. If only I could see

under their door the glowing bubble
the light comes from, the quick pulse

at the centre beating like concussion:
the hidden verb of their talk.

In a lit corner of the hall
I can see their two bodies bend

apart like a river forking.
Hear their neat footsteps pause

on the turning-point of the stairs.
An exact door clicks.

Then the dark house makes
untranslated language in the night:

pound and pound, pound,
overheard from my bed.

THE SEA CHILD

The sea was banging its crib.
It was rocking back and forth
in the small turmoil
of a child in a dark room alone.

For the sun had blown out for good
taking with it every light,
with no intention of coming back
without an apology. *But what is my body for
if it's not for you?*

The sea sulked.
It crouched and rippled
then lay sly as a plate watching
the sky, scanning its empty grey-blue walls

for a door that might open for you
to come in as if nothing had happened.
Intent on her face
the sea sat in the lap of the sky.
You fill the world when you're this close.

The sea talked, but only by watching
the other's mouth: a flickering blue
full of devices of light
it stole from the sky and pretended to own.

Slowly working at closing,
opening, closing,
the waves mouthed themselves
to make the words come alive.
But each dumb shape just lolled

without insisting,
like a dead tongue on a slab
with no real form of its own,
or stuttered at a whim of the wind.

So the sea led them in to the beach,
dreaming of the tenderness of milk,
then slammed and slammed,
each meek wave lifted, tucked under
and crushed on the stones.

It's that letting go I want.
To be loved and destroyed, loved
and destroyed. That letting go in which
I am washed away. But all she wanted

was to stand on the beach as if
it was solid rock. The sun
would enter the sea's blue-black dream,
lunging and shimmering,
and be right there in the moments after sleep,

coming, going and coming back all
on the same day. She wanted one word
held back to wait in a cry,
to be the tear that had to be wept

first, that would then fall
gigantic and multiple as rain.
She wanted to hear its placatory
consoling sounds, when joking together
they would both come, in a little while,

to tuck her in, the light between them
growing them together in a broad smile.
She wanted to fasten
their words together, to weave herself

into their voluble talk,
you moving, I moving inside you,
to be lost in the seamless whisper
through the window: the sound of waves
never completely breaking.

THE SWING

A push as light as a hat.
    Pointing your accurate legs,
full length on your back you rise

on loan to the sky.
    You've gone swimming way
over your head in air. Milkweed bursts

and drifts, so much white
    bleeds from the open pod
that light as a city of cream

you've begun to grow wide, to spill
    over the rim, to branch
like the edge of a cloud.

Trees arrive and open small green fans,
    a hill bends down
behind another hill. And here

again and again above you hangs
    the world turned upside-down,
the door you enter feet first

flush with the tops of trees,
    the blue floor where you walk
on the sky. You are now so high

that down the stairs in the morning
    you find the sun,
a tiny wafer of white, is rising

from an envelope there on the mat,
    a tree trembling
behind the house, dropping its bark:

two thin bare legs step through
　　　the narrow trunk. Hold on
to the toppling moment before it falls

Hi-Lili, Hi-Lili, Hi-Lo.
　　　But this is the toy of here and gone,
touchwood, shadowtouch, tip and run.

For all is out
　　　at the end of the swing
Hi-Lili, Hi-Lili, Hi-Lo.

The world repeats its scurry away.
　　　Don't ask me how I know.

NYMPHET

The sea moves in a sleeveless dress:
all its sudden girls' white arms up

over their heads wriggle out, huge jokes
explode in the level calm,

a handful of aces poured smack on the table.

The Rhyme of the Hatching Duck

She didn't have to learn to swim
In her smallest infancy
Adrift in warmest albumen
No larger than a pea.

Her egg was a tiny nursery.
It was a sea without a tide
A starry dark infinity
And she was safe inside.

Her wings were closed, her eyes were blind
Yet a single thought as undefined
As a wave upon the sea
Rippled the surface of her mind
And then broke free.

With all her force and strength combined
She struck a mighty peck
And through the dome her beak inclined
Like a mast upon a deck.

The broken skylight of the egg
Lay scattered all around:
A lonesome archipelago
And she as sad as helpless dough
Sat sticky on the ground.

She tried to get up on her feet
To lift her webby wings.
They all collapsed into a heap
Of useless flopping things.

Sound, light, colour, scent
But nothing to recognize.
Think of her excitement when
She found you with her eyes.

Let me tell you how she drifted once
in warm albumen, a spark of silver

floating in the dark.
She was skinless and indistinguishable,

the meeting-point of all
four corners of the compass

an emperor of emptiness inside-out
in her element.

As resistless as water
she flowed with no more idea of where

she might begin or end than a calendar
all in one colour or the sea.

But when time had strangely come
filling herself with herself

and feeling oddly large, bobbing
to the top she banged her head

splintering the seams of the sky.
Infinite egg lay scattered

lightly on the ground.
Her eyes fell on you with the hard

attentiveness of metal.
Now her webbed feet weave

idiotically across waste ground.
Flopping like spilled water a duck

chasing a brief thing
moving too quickly

thinks: this is my mother.

MOVING PICTURE

Impatient houselights go dim.
A red plush slanted floor runs down
to scenery blue-white as milk.

What's going to happen now? Another whole
eager world. Here everything tears open
an invitation. Green is a child

playing down there in front of the trees.
They stand straight up with the dark
authority of saints. It's the palest blue

circling overhead attentive as a mother
whose huge face holds the sun. Keep this
framed picture propped on a shelf (maybe

covered with a little dust): the light
from a distant theatre
the sky inside quietly pours out.

COSMOLOGY

When her face gazing down
at one time held a sun
people would tell each other stories

about how the earth spoke
in green details after a long silence,
about how the trees would come out

of doors to celebrate and stand around
in voluble groups outdoing themselves
stirring, fleshing, flowering.

People would get down on their knees
as it passed across the sky like a woman
moving from room to room in a house.

She sits down to comb her hair and she is
the incandescent centre,
the blue long-awaited letter torn open

to let us see its one shining point
of reference, and there in a cloudy system of worlds

the weather is clear.
It's late afternoon in early spring.
The light is falling on a certain tree.

EQUATOR

When she held your small heart tight as the equator,
she was immense. Houses bobbed up and down
around her as she turned in the bed of the world,
her body lifting and falling like the sea.

With one sweep of her hand, towns were wiped
from the face of the earth. She left the wrinkled
shore fine as a sheet. In propitious weather
her breath had the regularity of day.

It was then a touch of her finger was an earthquake
filmed in reverse. Towns reappeared. Bricks rose
into place, jumping from the sinking dust.
Lost days scattered on the floor were threaded

back like history on a knotted string. When her
arms once ringed the sky and drew
the circumference of everything in sight,
you stood like a little tower on her lap

balanced by the tip of her finger.

THE NARROW KISS

after Rilke

The wooded path takes an unfamiliar
swing to the left. Immediately
the sky is open for business.
The flat sea is wrinkling

its face, throws back its head in a laugh.
As if we had been children together
the blue water runs with me.
The horizon keeps up from a distance

like a song I don't know by heart.
An aching line reaches all the way
to remind me: this is where we went
taking a map that was only a wish.

It is where we were always together.
Come again into the open
inside of the fruit, into the white
inexhaustible milk. Come again into

the quick. It is where overnight,
following the gentlest law, the skin
also opened, where we were not surface
any longer but voluminous and sea-deep.

Where two mouths formed a narrow
kiss we slipped through, we swam
in the green room of ourselves breathing
the impossible breath of fish.

But now the sun is high and blurred.
The sea has stepped back into
a blue glimpse behind the trees. But you,

the water I see, your laughing voice,
your gestures touching the sand
still remind me of someone I know.

The Spectrum

What do you want me to say?
That you are as green as the eye can see?
That I am red for you alone,
blood-brother red?

What do you want me to say?
That in this soft yellow of two
small mouths, red and green
have never been more themselves?

That in this violent yellow
with red and green for a mouth
we fall on each other like meat?
Or with the delicacy of a leaf?

What do you want me to say?
That where red and green have touched
we may never untouch?
That in this ecstatic devouring
consuming and nourishing are the same?

THE ORIGIN OF THE SEXES
ACCORDING TO ARISTOPHANES

Fireworks – especially Catherine wheels
circled the sky. We spun out
head-over-heels, an elated shower
of lights. We had at least two heads,
four arms and legs and several tongues.
Spikes grew from the fingers of our
unclenched hands; a thousand forms burst
with a deafening report from our beating
hearts. Our high voices rolled
the length of the horizon for hours on end
without falling. We were blue touch-paper,
rings of hung mist, red-haloed chisel-points
in the dark. Shooting stars had nothing on our
full speed, forced landings in mid-air,
our perfect incendiary curves.
Our ascent to heaven would surely
take place at any moment; and the rest
of the world backed away, for who
can embrace a fire? *This perfection must stop!*
A god stepped in. The swift parting slice
of an axe. Since then the lights have dimmed,
and we must hobble on the earth on two legs.

THE FLOOD

Silly even to think closing
the doors would do any good.
So when the water rose
between the tiles, we thought ok
let's put everything up on slightly
higher shelves, slip bricks under
the corners of the cooker, jack
up the legs of the table. It was then
the river grew large, began running
distractedly like a wounded dog
smelling sweetly of rain, rankly
of earth, poured over the threshold,
flooded the floor, tossing leaves,
a tennis ball of fluorescent green,
the muddled ruins of a coat,
lapped and sucked the furniture,
left foam in the closed drawers.
A pool formed in the dented
crown of a hat. The stuffed chairs became
oddly dark. We could hear it
breathing from the second floor,
a sound of dull concussion beating
quietly in an empty cupboard.

We slept close to it like a heart
at night, an eyelid covering an eye.
How did we know it would be day
inside the room and outside,
filling the corners, the sky and all
available space? Nor could we plan

the way the house would melt
and lose its form, ceilings floating
wide-open and apart, walls
sagging window-frames out of square,
nor how still the varied contents of
the house would lie in new
and strange positions looking up,
an ebb-tide pointing out a wreck;
nor afterwards, on the table,
how carefully the sun would pick
a few cups and spoons, mark
new shadows precisely on the cloth,
and speak their meticulous names.

FISHING

Fishing in an old wound
where, for all I know, I am
the fish, mouth airy as a cave,
waiting vertical and still in the dark.

Exactly in the centre is the red hook
baited with succinct meat.
Fluttering mouth caught on the long
illusion, I suck hope against hope.

Whose red badge do I trail home,
nodding, an idiot in my skin,
tilted as a fish travelling on its side
out of true? The way back is streaked

with red. There I am again and again
throwing the trolling line into the wound.
It keeps flapping open

like brilliantly white curtains
blowing from an upstairs window,
like a baby held in the air,
as though the four drowned walls

of the kitchen boasted a high-tide mark,
as though the ceiling had forgotten its
predictable height. Is it enough?

The stiff chairs improvise at the table;
a skin of milk wrinkles on the cup.
Clouds blow over, stunted
shadows moving under an even light.

41

SMALL ANTI-DEPRESSANT

Clouds indolently loiter,
fitting the sea like a lid.
A stunned tongue locked

in a bell makes no more sound
than an insect's trapped banging
against the paper shade of a lamp.

It feels good to unbolt the window
to release a huge headlong bee.

LOST PROFILE

You took my face in your hands.
You took it to a quiet place
inside. There you traced it
with your finger. A white

square window thrown open pierced
a darkened room. Speaking quietly,
details packed into the distance.
Each instant touched on a blue,

turning to look, began a sky,
let through the line of a hill.
Slowly-forming, a tree
stood in the sky and broke

into colour. A country was hiding
its view like a profile shying away.
One day you say: Your face has changed.
Yes. You are making it happen.

Fruit Tree

Standing there all you can do is wait
for me now, your bare branches holding
nothing in the air
reach out empty-handed as a beggar.

You have dropped all of your fruit
irretrievably to the ground.
In bunches of warm red, taut and wrinkled,
the round lolling skins lie together
like bodies touching in bed, they would almost burst.

But they are so far below the branches,
quite out of reach. Your broken wrists
going off at angles and dead-end limbs
you can only stand and hang.
You cannot bend to reach the fruit again.

In fact, you'll never have it back
unless I come, because, beloved beggar,
you've given away to me your very skin,
you've lost your eyes and arms.
Your face and hands now all belong to me.

And there you wait sheared off and blind,
as smooth and empty as the body of a jar,

which as I come, and slowly pouring, fill it –
in place of handles seems to grow hands.

THE SUN ON A ROAD

Determined that I should go
along an open sunlit road pinned down
and crossed and crossed with piercing marks

where blossoming trees throw sharp
black blossoming shadows
I saw him with a shining whip

lean through the air. I saw it climb
above his head, curl back, the soundless
black flash burning like a nerve,

and a thin white body stretching out
striped with leafy light and dark.

LOOKING FOR THE HEART

The small intelligent places
know where it is kept.
The cushions all tilt up like stones
disclosing squares of bleached white grass,
a nest of cellophane, a broken
match, the body of a moth.
I slide my fingers down
inside the arm, along the back:
a paperclip, a yellow pencil stub.
Somewhere in the house
a pea is beating quietly, remotely,
under sixteen mattresses hiding
in the dark, a kiss living
in a box on top of the wardrobe.

While I rush and shine in a rage
of looking, bright as an engine
doing a thousand revolutions per minute
in neutral, blithe as a toy boat
sailing straight into a paper bag,
I'm down among the lost
long lanes, the backs of cupboards,
the overcast dusk under beds,
digging into the soft
insides of drawers, among
the unpaired socks, the hard belts;
deep in the wet weeds, my hands
encounter a snail. Yet the drawers
stick out with nothing wrong, silent
as tongues at the clinic, books lie
unpiled in ruins, shelves desolate as streets.

Now ten feet tall with a tiny head,
hollow as the Tin Woodsman, and echoing
like the spaces under a bridge,
I'm clanking down the stairs, one foot out
in front of the other, lifting each
puppet wrist in turn. I'm entering
the room as reluctantly as a party.
A door you can't argue with, a carpet
flinging a low sidelong glance.
It's either the crumpled curtains standing
by the window or the utter
silence of a chair. A smooth polished table
keeps me circling at arm's length.

MAP

Even if you hold your breath and hide
thinly between books, the red covers lift
in and out just enough to see.
A small cry growing inside the folds
is saying *open, open.* I want you

unfolded on the floor, hills peeled back,
a white valley falling open,
a river miles below sending fine blue lines
delicately down the sides of mountains
puckered and tan as skin.

I want to know the way you have
of stretching out in arbitrary green
a plump shape odd
as the profile of a dog,
the tendency of coves to let
the ocean sink its fingers in,
the longing of peninsulas
when they're setting out to meet
another shore, but never do,
the way volcanic islands float
like joy. I want to understand
the words hanging loosely from the shore,
a black fringe dangling
sideways from a skirt.

But becoming strange along the maze
of coupled shapes, a flattened yellow
jigsawed to a mauve, a blue place hugging
a pink place with a black dot, geography
oversimplifies you.

The sea, a thin curve in a trance,
barely moves on the page,
and paths . . . paths everywhere stamped flat
shrink into the hidden dossier
their fine print your unreadable invisible life.

My Nights in Cupid's Palace

Down a narrow hall ending
in a drop of light,
velvet rooms lead
to velvet rooms. Silently the vivid food

appears again, well-lit, on tables laid
by hands without arms
lavish fingers without hands,

asking to be touched.
Help Yourself. My mouth is soft
as water, as I think — *Yes.*

Alone in this flimsy tent,
on the far edge of a field, my mind
an embryonic curl
grows very small until it goes out.

FINDING MY BEARINGS

Such intricate
navigational equipment.
A search of the black sky

for the Pole Star. Soundings
to establish a safe depth.
Sailing in the dark up

the empty estuary, shining hotel
corridors with static
electricity in each doorknob.

Never go down teeteetum teeteetum
if you don't go down with me.
Why are the little roads

to your secret address so faint?
The *A to Z* of your smile without
getting lost. Its turnings and

mysterious co-ordinates.
Let's look it up
in the index under S:

Something Circus
Something Crescent
Something Close

THE BLACKBERRY

Your face is a cipher when your smile
splays out into the many

double directions a child takes on a walk,
twirling a stem of grass in an erratic

circle of two minds
Do I want this? Do I want this?

The smile on its way to your face
dawdles, lost in thought.

It is stopping to pick blackberries
on the hot path. The dangling

things on the verge of having
must hold still under the leaves.

Lift the berry slowly
between your thumb and forefinger

so it slips off whole from the stem,
all of its loose possibilities

you softly swallow intact in your mouth,
the round knob of syllables

making one word that sounds exactly right.
But its double kiss, thicketed and warm,

is a little white lie
cuffed in fur. Hard losing itself

in soft, fusty and sweet, like hearing
your own voice all wrong.

Smash it like the toy you didn't want
against a wall. If you could only

hold everything dark-coloured on your tongue
forever without breaking:

little reds becoming black
scripts written on your lips.

ACCOMPLICE

Begin by letting him be the word
you keep hidden under your tongue,
while you wait there innocent

as an envelope with a letter growing quietly
inside it. He'll tear open and unfold
the whole of it, come straight out

to meet you, leaping three steps at a time,
the screen-door banging behind him,
with a hundred demon arms and a smile.

Let him come out entirely himself, complete as a sperm,
bright as a moment in the mind.
He's the secret accomplice who sleeps with you.

All night, sharp as light, he'll be alive
inside the dark jack-in-the-box of your sleep,
prying an eyelid to spring the sky

open in the morning when you blink.
Blue will appear alert at the window, jump
to attention when he holds it up to the light.

The room, in a hurry to assemble
in perfect perspective, will throw its walls, floors,
corners together, so it stands straight up,

just like that, when you get out of bed. Now he's
beginning the words you hear in your mouth
coming in a sharp torrent of syllables.